Basic Bowl Turning

with

Judy Ditmer

D1397800

Schiffer Publishing Ltd

77 Lower Valley Road, Atglen, PA 19310

DEDICATION

This book is dedicated to Evelyn Snyder and to Betty Scarpino, in appreciation of their abiding friendship.

ACKNOWLEDGEMENTS

I would like to thank the following people: John Sherman for getting the ball rolling (or the bowl turning); Liam O'Neill for teaching me how to make a nice shaving; Al Stirt, Palmer Sharpless, George Kridler, Russ Haidet, and Mark and Hilarie Burhans for cheering me on; and Denver Ulery for making such a nice lathe for me.

Also, deep appreciation to each of the forty-two individuals who made my Lathe Fund Project a success.

Finally, I would especially like to thank Alix French for her early and continuing support and encouragement; and of course, Mom, for typing and about a million other things.

Copyright © 1994 by Judy Ditmer
Library of Congress Catalog Number: 94-65624

All rights reserved. No part of this work may be reproduced or used in any forms or by any means graphic, electronic or mechanical, including photocopying or information storage and retrieval systems without written permission from the copyright holder.

Printed in China
ISBN: 0-88740-627-0

We are interested in hearing from authors
 with book ideas on related topics.

Published by Schiffer Publishing Ltd.
77 Lower Valley Road
Atglen, PA 19310
Please write for a free catalog.
This book may be purchased from the publisher.
Please include $2.95 postage.
Try your bookstore first.

CONTENTS

INTRODUCTION

My grandmother loved beautiful dishes of all kinds, but especially bowls. I remember many special ones. A delicate glass bowl sat on the kitchen table, filled with pansies floating in water; there was always a lidded ceramic dish in the refrigerator, full of fruit. A cut crystal bowl occupied the kitchen counter, and contained our favorite candies. A handpainted, turned-wood bowl from Norway stood on the coffee table during the holidays, filled to the rim with Christmas cards. So I suppose my delight in bowls of all kinds is a natural heritage.

When I was younger I worked in clay. I made, among many other things, bowls. I liked to do sculptures, but there was a special magic in throwing: shaping the spinning lump of clay into a graceful container.

When I first began to make bowls of wood, it seemed to me the most magical thing I'd ever done. Until then I had built cabinets and similar projects of wood, but had done virtually no lathe work. The process of turning, especially turning bowls, where the designing and the making of a piece can be so completely integrated in time and space, was wonderful.

I love a well-made bowl. I love the idea of a bowl: the potential it embodies to contain the items, the moments, the nourishment of our lives. In a book about African art I read about a tribe which uses a certain type of low stool to sit upon during many of the activities of everyday life. There are many stools made, of somewhat varying designs, which are meant for use and are ordinary, almost invisible, parts of daily life. But there are also special stools made, stools which are never to be sat upon. In learning about this I began to understand the sculptural, "non-functional" bowls I had begun to make. Like the ceremonial stools, they were an acknowledgement of the great meaning which inheres in the most ordinary objects we use each day.

THE PURPOSE OF THIS BOOK

My purpose in this book is to take you step-by-step through the process of making a bowl, from cutting the green log, through roughing-out and drying the bowl, to finish turning the dry bowl and completing the foot of the piece. My aim is to show the whole process, and to address in some detail problems which may arise at various points.

I won't attempt to tell you every possible way of doing each step, or even all or most of the ways I myself use. I will try to give you enough information about the methods I am describing so that you will be able to follow through and do them.

There are many ways of doing most of the steps involved in bowl turning. The omission of certain chucks, tools, jigs and techniques from this book doesn't mean I don't use them myself or consider them legitimate. It only means that space is limited. Consider this book a starting place. You'll go on to discover new options and with experience will find that some suit you better than others.

In the meantime, make a few bowls to get started. I hope you'll find the process as satisfying as I do.

EQUIPMENT & SUPPLIES

Equipment

You can turn bowls on almost any lathe. If your machine is large and heavy-duty you can make large bowls; if it is not then you must limit the size of your work accordingly. Don't try to turn a piece of wood which is too large and heavy for your machine to handle. Bigger isn't intrinsically better. What matters is how well you do what you do, and that you don't get injured doing it!

If you don't have a lathe yet, I would suggest you try out as many as you can. Give considerable thought to the types of turning you plan to do. In general, for bowl turning, important features would include heavy-duty bearings and spindle, an easily adjustable tool rest, enough distance from spindle to bed to do a decent-sized bowl, variable speed starting at around 300-400 rpm (many if not most lathes on the market have speed ranges geared to spindle turning, which are far too fast for much bowl turning), and a reversing switch.

There is a huge variety of chucks available for holding work on the lathe. Many are very impressive engineering achievements (and many are not!), and are priced accordingly. You don't need any of them to turn a bowl. In this book I will show you how to turn a bowl using only a standard faceplate to turn the piece, and a shop-made chuck/jig to hold the completed bowl for turning the foot.

Materials

Bowls can be made from almost any wood, but hardwoods are easier to turn than softwoods. Often they are more attractive and are generally more durable in use. You can frequently find logs already cut into convenient, short pieces where a neighborhood tree has been cut down. I won't even attempt here to address the cutting down of trees. It is a complicated and dangerous undertaking (that's why it's going to cost you a thousand dollars to have that old four-foot-diameter behemoth next to the house taken down!). You should attempt it only if you are very experienced with a chainsaw and trained in the techniques and dangers of tree removal.

If you don't own a chainsaw and have no desire to become a lumberjack, there are other sources of material. You can certainly turn bowls from dry lumber purchased at a lumberyard or sawmill, although clearly this will limit the size of your bowls. Still, even if you are limited to using 2" or 3" thick boards from your local lumberyard, there are innumerable design possibilities within this framework. More and more lumberyards and mills are beginning to carry wood cut with the turner in mind. There are many mail-order sources for turning stock, both green and dry, in as many species as you can think of. It is possible to purchase blocks several inches thick for bowl turning. Woodworking publications are good places to begin looking for sources; they will carry current ads from wood suppliers. Work in the way which seems most appropriate for you.

Supplies and Miscellaneous

Additional items you will need include a variable speed, reversing drill, sanding discs and a supply of sandpaper in several grits, rubber cement for gluing up sanding discs, screws and so forth. These are discussed in more detail at the appropriate places in the text.

Turning Tools

The tools I use to turn a bowl. Top to bottom, the tools and a brief description of their uses (discussed in greater depth in the text):

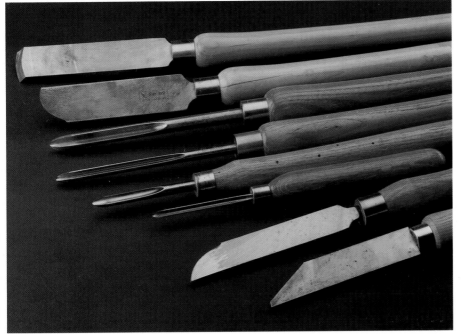

Two large, heavy scrapers, used for some minor interior shaping but primarily for delicate clean-up cuts on the inside of the bowl. One is ground with a very shallow curve, for use on slightly curving surfaces; the other has a tighter curve for use on closer curves in the bowl. Thick, heavy scrapers work best, as their mass will help eliminate vibration problems in use.

1/2" and 3/8" deep-flute bowl gouges, used for primary turning and shaping of the bowl, and sometimes for finish cuts. The deep flute of these gouges makes them especially useful in bowl work. They can remove more wood while roughing out the bowl, they are easier to control, and when ground back on the sides they can be used for a wider variety of cuts than shallower gouges.

3/8" and 1/4" spindle gouges. These are used for finish, detail, and texturing cuts on the outside, foot, and rim of the bowl. They are also ground back on the sides to a "fingernail" shape, giving a long point which aids in making precise detail and finishing cuts, and a longer side edge which is useful in certain finishing cuts.

Two medium scrapers. These are used exclusively for finishing cuts, usually called "shear-scraping", on the outside of the bowl. One is ground in a convex curve, for use on concave surfaces. The other is ground straight and at an angle, for use on convex surfaces.

SHARPENING

Sharpening Equipment

Tools can be sharpened several ways. There are many kinds of grinders on the market--wet and dry, horizontal and vertical, fast and slow, large and small. Tools can be ground on belt sanders and disc sanders as well. At present I am using a small, 3450 rpm bench grinder which I purchased at Odd Lots for $25. The only modification I have made to it (other than replacing the switch when it wore out) is to replace the coarse wheels that came on the machine. On one side I now have a rubber-bonded abrasive wheel. This is used to smooth and polish the rough steel of the bevels of tools that have just come off the grinding wheel. This rough steel would tend to mar the surface of the wood as it follows the cut. On the other side is a pink wheel made with a bonding agent that allows the particles of abrasive to break off more readily as the tool is ground. This helps to keep the tool from overheating as quickly, and prevents loading of the wheel with particles of steel. Overheating and loading are common problems with the coarse grey wheels that typically come with grinders. I don't actually know the grit of my pink wheel, but I imagine it's 100 or so. The number isn't as important as learning to use the thing properly. These pink wheels (sometimes they are white) are readily available in many tool catalogs and woodworking stores.

I should explain that my fantasy sharpening set-up differs somewhat from my actual one. In fact, I've recently purchased several items with which I will add to it. When all is set up, I will have the following: a coarse wheel (for re-shaping tools where a lot of steel has to be removed), my trusty pink wheel (for general grinding), a rubber-bonded abrasive wheel (for smoothing and polishing bevels) and several felt and stitched buffing wheels with various compounds (for finer polishing of the bevel). I will also have a 10" ultra-slow-speed, very fine grit water-cooled wheel for very fine shaping and grinding. And what-the-hey, as soon as I've got a few hundred dollars with no better claim on them, I'm planning to have one of those three-quarter-horse, slow speed, heavy, sitting-on-its-own-stand, **quiet**, quality bench grinders...lovely things. But for the moment, it's my reliable old $25 Odd Lots special.

The point of all this is that you don't need to spend a fortune on a lot of fancy equipment to do your sharpening. I've done a **lot** of turning--and I earn a living at it--doing all my grinding on the simple grinder described, making everything from tops and pens to earrings and sculptural bowls. That should tell you something.

If you currently have no sharpening equipment, I suggest you purchase a slow speed (1725 rpm or slower) bench grinder, and put a pink or white wheel on one side and a rubber-bonded abrasive wheel on the other. Then practice sharpening and turning until your work and increasing skills tell you what elaborations on this setup you may require. Mount a can in front of the grinder and fill it part way with water. When doing extensive re-grinding as on a new tool, or when sharpening small tools, you need to dip the tool frequently to prevent overheating. If the tool gets too hot, it will soften the steel and the tool won't hold an edge. Be sure your grinder is well lighted. If you can't see what you're doing, you won't be able to get a good edge. I have mounted a swing-arm lamp near the grinder so that it can easily be moved into the position which best illuminates the operation. You may also wish to use a magnifying lamp, headpiece, etc.

Finally, *DO NOT* use any grinder without wearing a face shield! There is a real danger of sparks or bits of flying metal and grit. Grinding wheels do occasionally break apart, and if this happens the little "guards" provided on the grinder may prove inadequate to protect your eyes and face.

The only other thing you need to start is a small, unmounted hard Arkansas stone, ceramic hone or diamond hone (flat) for raising a burr on scrapers, and possibly a small slipstone for removing the burr on the inside of the flute on gouges.

That will be enough to get you started.

Sharpening Technique

Mastering sharpening requires practice. An obvious statement, it would seem. Yet I have found a beginning turner will often work very hard at a particular cut, sweating bullets as it were, to get it right--with an improperly ground or dull tool. Much of the difficulty experienced by beginning students with turning is due to dull or poorly-shaped tools.

You should expect to spend some time working at sharpening. At first, you may not really be able to tell a good edge from a poor one, so you will have to keep at it. Try to pay attention to what is happening while you are using the tool. You will gradually learn to tell what the problem may be with a particular tool, whether it's a dull edge, a bevel that is too short or long, an improperly shaped bevel, or something else.

You need to acquire a "feel" for sharpening so you can grind the tool as needed in any given situation. "Numbers", that is, angles, length of bevels, and so on, are of limited usefulness. They are only general guidelines at best, since inevitably you will have a situation for which the textbook case doesn't work, and you'll have to change the tool to accommodate the reality. So I will try to state the principles or theory behind the instructions for sharpening a certain way, including how the tool is supposed to work. That way, you will be able not only to sharpen the tool, but also modify it when necessary.

The following are specific instructions for sharpening each tool. General principles of sharpening are discussed as well.

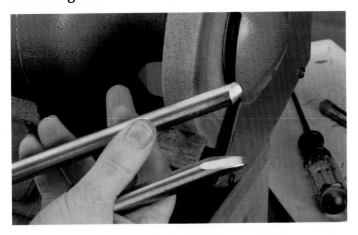

The larger deep-fluted bowl gouge. At the top is the grind on the tool as it comes from the factory; below is the modified grind I use. This is a side view.

Top view of the two grinds...

and bottom view.

To make the initial modification, hold the top of the tool against the grinder and move it slowly up and down, rocking it slightly in this same direction. This establishes the profile shown in the top photo on the previous page. Grind the sides by moving the tool back and forth sideways as shown until the excess steel is removed. The tool shown has already been ground, but the principle is the same. Just be sure to hold the tool steadily--i.e., in this position, don't twist the handle or you will round the bevel over and never get a sharp edge. You are grinding the bevel, not the edge. Keep the tool in the same position with regard to the wheel. Watch for tiny sparks to appear at the edge. This means the bevel has reached the top surface of the tool to create the edge. Don't rush it by leaning the edge into the wheel.

You don't need to push the tool into the wheel. This will cause overheating and will make it harder to shape the tool properly. Hold the tool firmly, and gently move it across the wheel. Let the grinder do its job.

Continue along the side, and blend into the bevel at the tip of the tool by swinging the handle around gradually...

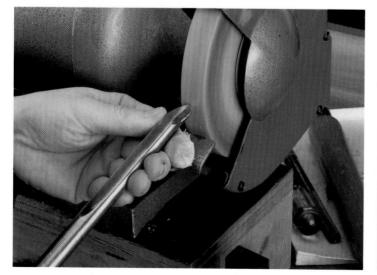

continuing across the tip...

and onto the bevel...

of the other side. While grinding the tip, the tool handle will be higher to keep the bevel from becoming too long. If the angle of the bevel at the tip is too acute, that is, if the blade is too thin, it will be impossible to follow the inside curve of the bowl.

While grinding the sides, the handle will be held lower to keep the edge more or less straight across the grinding wheel.

Notice that I am grinding the tool "free-hand". This sometimes looks intimidating to beginners, but it is not so hard to learn and is a superior way to sharpen. Actually, my hand is resting on the tool rest, and the tool is resting on my hand, which thus becomes an infinitely-adjustable tool rest-- one which responds immediately to my mental commands (no wrenches or levers to operate!) and can hold the tool in any desired position. No mechanical jig or rest will ever be able to do that!

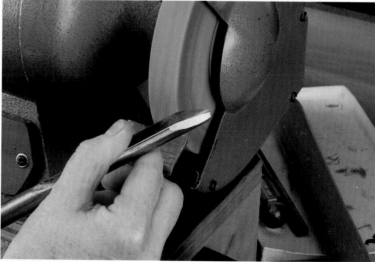

The freshly-ground tool.

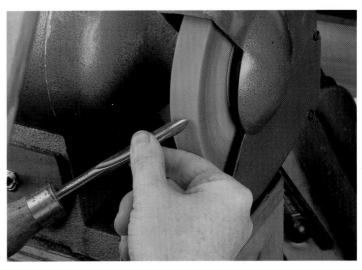

The smaller bowl gouge is ground in the same manner.

I should mention that the nominal and actual sizes of these gouges as listed in some catalogs do not always agree. There are usually three sizes. Here, I will use the small and medium of the three, and those are the ones I would suggest to you to start with. The largest size is useful in two cases: for removing very large amounts of wood (possible only with green wood and a powerful lathe), and for lighter cuts where the mass of the tool can overcome vibration problems caused by a long overhang from the toolrest. You can easily get along with the two smaller sizes.

moving toward the tip...

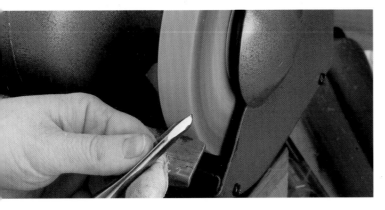

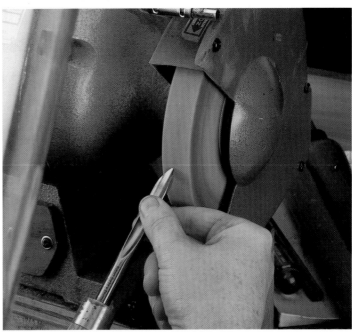

The "fingernail" grind on the shallow (spindle) gouge. This is the 3/8" gouge.

across, and...

Begin at the outside edge, gradually...

blending...

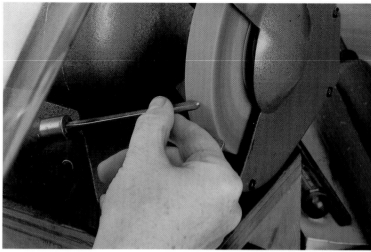

along into a smooth bevel all the way around.

    Note that as you sharpen the outer edge, the handle is nearly horizontal, and is gradually lowered as you approach the tip, to keep the bevel long. On this tool, the nice long bevel and thin edge at the tip of the tool allow it to be used effectively for precision and finish cuts.

Begin on one end...

The freshly-ground tool.

blending into the tip...

The small spindle gouge is ground the same way.

and around to the other end. Be careful when grinding small tools like this one not to overheat the edge.

The finished grind.

The large curved scraper. Begin grinding along the outside edge. Be sure to hold the tool steady, with the bevel against the wheel and not rocking as you move the handle around. You don't want to round over the bevel. Gradually swing the handle around...

keeping the tool steady as you complete the curve.

The bevel. It doesn't have to be perfect, but note that it is nice and concave up to the edge, not rounded over.

Always remember, you are grinding the bevel, not the edge. Thinking of it this way will help you to avoid rounding the bevel, which spoils the edge. The edge is created where the bevel meets the surface of the tool. If you attend properly to the bevel, the edge will take care of itself.

I use a fairly long bevel on these scrapers. The thinner edge makes it easier to raise and maintain a good cutting burr. Most scrapers come with a very blunt end--far too much so for practical use. I nearly always re-grind a new scraper to lengthen the bevel. This sometimes entails removing a lot of steel, so get comfortable, fill your water container, and use the time to ruminate a bit on such matters as interest you.

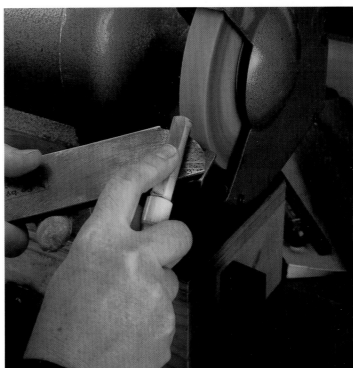

In using the scrapers, the cutting is actually done with a minute wire edge, or burr, which is raised along the edge of the tool. Since I find the wire edge raised by the grinding wheel is not always completely smooth, I rework it: First, I rub a flat hand-held stone (this is a ceramic hone; you can also use a small, fine diamond hone or a hard Arkansas stone) back and forth across the top of the tool to remove the burr left by grinding. The hone must be held flat against the tool.

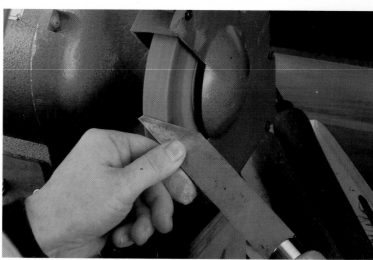

Next, holding the hone almost flat across the concavity of the bevel (it's actually tilted very slightly toward the top edge), draw it around the tool edge once or twice...

across the tool.

to create a new, clean burr along the edge. This may take some practice. You can feel a good wire edge by drawing your thumb outward across the top of the tool. You will actually feel it gently scraping your skin, as it will scrape the wood.

You can generally renew the burr once or twice, by repeating the above procedure (starting with the hone on the top of the tool), before it is necessary to return to the grinder and renew the bevel.

It should look something like this.

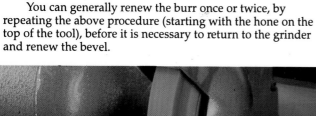

The smaller, straight scraper is prepared the same way. Grind a straight, clean bevel...

Draw the hone across the flat top of the tool...

and then across the edge to raise the burr.

To reiterate some of the principles to keep in mind while sharpening:

Grind the bevel, not the edge. When the bevel meets the tool surface, the edge will appear. This can be seen as it occurs by watching for tiny sparks to appear at the edge as you grind.

Move the handle of the tool in whatever direction necessary to follow the contour of the bevel of the tool. Keep the bevel in good contact with the wheel.

Keep the tool cool. That's another good reason for using the hand and fingers as your tool rest. If the tool is uncomfortably warm to your skin, it may be very close to burning, especially if it is a very small tool. Dip the tool frequently in the water cup to keep it cool. Don't let it get hot enough to change color--if it does, you may have drawn the temper, or made the steel too soft to hold an edge.

Use gradual, smooth, steady movements as you grind. Let the grinding wheel do the work; you don't need to lean the tool into the stone.

Practice. Practice. Practice.

☙ Roughing out the Bowl

This is a small beech log which has been cut for some time. Note the cracking on the end and the fungus growth. Sometimes a log like this is too far gone to turn, if the wood has gotten too soft or punky. However, it is surprising how often there is usable wood just below these surface flaws. You can't tell until you cut it.

Note the piece is supported with small wedges of wood. This will keep it from rocking back and forth or getting away from me as I cut. I am cutting in several inches from the end, to get past the cracking and other damage.

A Safety Reminder

Woodturning can be dangerous. Although this book is intended for beginning turners, it does assume a certain basic familiarity with woodworking tools and processes. Be certain that you know how to use your tools and equipment in a safe manner. Read and understand the information that came with your machines.

A chainsaw is a powerful and useful tool, but it can be deadly. If you are not familiar with its safe use, you should begin by turning smaller, prepared stock or having a friend who is well-versed in chainsaw use prepare the material at this stage.

Obtain competent instruction in chainsaw use and safety before you begin.

Keep safety in mind--the front of your mind--at all times. Don't use any tool in a manner inconsistent with its intended purpose. Always wear eye and face protection, and use some form of dust collection or filtering mask.

Specific safety pointers or concerns in the text are identified with a

PLEASE PAY ATTENTION TO THEM.

The wood inside is still sound; in fact it has developed some interesting spalting lines. Spalting refers to the dark lines that are created by fungus as the wood ages. It actually denotes the beginning of decay, but in the early stages the wood is still sound. The effect of spalting can be very dramatic and pleasing.

Measure the diameter through the thickest part of the log. This will be the distance across the top of the bowl, so...

Make a line through the center of the log. This should be the pith or growth center, not the geographic or measured center.

you'll transfer this measurement to the side of the log...

Carry the line down the side, matching to the pith line you've drawn on the other end. Most wood tends to split more easily at the pith, so you don't want this part to be used in the bowl.

and cut the piece to this length.

Cut the log in half along its length. Note that the log is carefully supported with wood wedges so it will stay in place as I cut. Make this cut with the log on its side so that you are cutting with the grain--that is, along the axis of the log. If you try to cut the log on end you'll be cutting across the end grain, which is difficult, and is unsafe.

This gives two pieces from which bowls can be turned.

If you will not be roughing out the bowl right away, you should coat the ends with a sealer. This prevents checking, which can begin almost immediately with some woods. The sealer slows down the moisture loss which causes this checking. I am using a water based wax emulsion designed for this purpose. Several brands are available. Most wood-working stores will have some available. Latex paint can also be used, but is less effective.

Be advised that this treatment will only "hold" the wood for a short time. You will need to mount the piece on the lathe as soon as possible and rough it out into a thick bowl shape for further drying. If you leave it in large pieces like the one pictured two things will happen. First, the wood, being wet, will continue to decay, sooner or later becoming too rotten to use. Second, and despite coating, it will continue to lose moisture unevenly and thus will crack.

Briefly, what happens is that as wood dries it shrinks. A large piece will lose moisture more quickly at the outside surfaces. Since they are drying (and therefore shrinking) around a core which is still wet (therefore not shrinking), cracks will appear and expand. Your lovely hunk of log will be spoiled. (I, of course, being an Experienced Professional Woodturner, never allow this to happen to my Well-Managed Wood Supply. Heh-Heh).

Cut the corners off the log...

To prepare the piece for the lathe, you must first locate the center so you can attach the faceplate, which will hold the piece to the lathe. Measure across from corner to corner and mark the center.

to take it to an octagonal shape. This will save you the very bumpy operation of cutting this material off on the lathe. Also, unless your lathe is very large, you will likely need to cut these corners for clearance over the lathe bed.

Repeat at several points.

The center of the resulting mark is (more or less) the center of the blank. Be advised that this "geographic" center is not necessarily the weight center of the piece. This means the piece may be out of balance when you put it on the lathe. Therefore it is best to start out with blanks which are smaller than the measured capacity of the lathe, because the off-balance blank may be too much for the lathe.

Hold the faceplate over the center you've established.

Tap the screws into the wood a bit with a hammer. Once the screws bite the wood, they'll stay in place while you begin to drive them in. I use 1 1/4" long screws. This will be the top of the bowl so the screw holes are in the wood that will be turned away from the interior of the bowl.

Drive the screws in. I use the square-drive type, as they are less prone to aggravating slippage while being driven. I use a high-torque, slow speed drill as a driver.

The faceplate is mounted.

16

Mount the piece on the lathe.

SAFETY TIP

Check for clearance by turning the piece all the way around by hand, before turning on the lathe.

One corner is hitting the bed. I mark this corner and remove the assembly from the lathe.

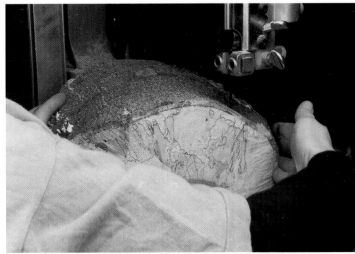

After removing the faceplate I take the piece to the band saw and cut off enough of the offending corner for the piece to clear the lathe bed.

Whenever you remove a piece from the faceplate, and will be mounting it again for further work, you must remount it the same way. Many faceplates have asymmetrically spaced holes so that they can only be replaced the same way. If your faceplate has symmetrically drilled holes make a mark somewhere on the rim. Then you can transfer that marking to the blank so you will be able to remount it in the same position.

The piece is re-mounted on the faceplate and the lathe.

SAFETY TIP

You may wish to bring the tailstock up for extra support, especially for the initial roughing out which can be a bit, well, rough. Also if there is any doubt as to the soundness of the wood, you should use the tailstock. Even fairly long screws can be pulled out of the wood if it is at all punky or soft. If the wood is obviously defective, don't use it!

In this case the wood is quite sound and the bowl is not especially large or out-of-balance, so the tailstock support isn't needed. So! At last I have begun, using the larger bowl gouge, to round up the blank.

Continue cutting from the center out.

Begin to create a flat bottom.

 **SAFETY TIP**

Always check before you turn on the lathe to make sure the speed is slow enough for safe operation. A rough piece of wood like this will always be out of balance initially. If you start up the lathe at high speed, the piece can tear loose from the faceplate, and you may be injured. At the least, your machine will be badly shaken up. You should begin roughing out a piece with your lathe speed at the lowest setting; you can increase the speed gradually as the piece becomes round and more balanced. Always wear a full face shield! Pieces of bark or wood can and often do fly off the lathe at incredible speeds.

After positioning the tool rest, it is very important to check for clearance by rotating the wood by hand through a full 360 degree turn. You must be certain the wood will not hit the rest. Also check that the tool rest is tightened down snugly wherever it adjusts.

After a few cuts, stop the lathe and check that the piece is not loosening from the faceplate. Place your fingers across the juncture of the faceplate and the wood and give the wood a sharp whack in front. If it is loosening you will be able to feel it at the faceplate. Tighten or remount if necessary.

Continue until there is a level flat foot an inch or two larger than your small faceplate.

Continue cutting outward from the foot and around the side.

This is what the tool looks like as it cuts. Note that it is the long edge, just left of the tip, which is doing the cutting. The bevel just next to the tip is rubbing the cut surface as it travels behind the edge.

 **SAFETY TIP**

This rubbing of the bevel is an important feature of a successful cut. If the bevel isn't rubbing, the gouge will have a great tendency to dig into the wood, sometimes causing a very dramatic and abrupt grab. This can injure the tool, the bowl, the lathe, or you!

With practice and a sufficiently powerful lathe, you can remove a lot of wood at a pass with this tool. This is nice when roughing out a lot of bowls. But don't get carried away. Take your time at first and learn how to make the cut properly. Use slow speeds on the lathe. If you are having difficulty, turn the lathe off and rotate the wood by hand as you attempt to make the cut. This way you can see and understand exactly what is happening at the edge. This is always a good practice when learning a new cut or the use of a new tool.

 SAFETY TIP

Always keep your arms and hands behind the plane of the tool rest. Otherwise part of your hand may be pulled into the rotation and caught between the rest and the spinning wood. This can cause devastating injury, especially when the wood is rough like this.

You may be able to increase the lathe speed as the bowl becomes round. Leave the flat at the base of the bowl for mounting a faceplate to turn the interior.

As I get rid of more of the irregularity of the rough piece, I begin to shape the bowl. Although I am cutting a fair amount of material at this point, the cut is a reasonably safe one, if done properly. Remember I am cutting with the long edge, left of the center (tip) of the tool. Should the edge dig in, causing a "grab", the tool handle will be yanked in a sharp counter-clockwise direction, but will not be jerked upwards into my face, as can happen when cutting at the tip of a tool which is conventionally ground. The left hand is holding the tool down against the rest. The right is controlling direction, depth etc., with handle movements.

and blending into the convex part of the bowl. A large movement of my right hand (at the end of the long handle) results in small movement of the business end of the gouge, giving me great control.

I always make a long handle for bowl gouges. It is very useful in controlling both the quality of the cut and the shape of the turned piece. In this sequence of photos, notice how the long tool handle provides leverage and control. I begin at the foot...

sweeping outward for a concave curve next to the foot...

The curve near the foot is roughed out. There is considerable tear-out, especially on the end grain from the very aggressive roughing-out cut with the large gouge.

I switch to the smaller bowl gouge, and taking a lighter cut, continue rounding toward the rim.

The surface is still quite rough at this stage because of the somewhat punky nature of the spalted wood. But I think I'll be able to get a good surface with finishing cuts.

I will do one more cut to level the surface, establish a nice smooth curve, and remove a few imperfections in the wood. This is done...

SAFETY TIP

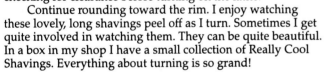

Move the tool rest closer to the work as you go, always checking for clearance before turning on the lathe.

Continue rounding toward the rim. I enjoy watching these lovely, long shavings peel off as I turn. Sometimes I get quite involved in watching them. They can be quite beautiful. In a box in my shop I have a small collection of Really Cool Shavings. Everything about turning is so grand!

in one long, smooth

sweeping

The basic bowl shape is established.

cut, from foot to rim. Notice how the handle sweeps back and forth as necessary to keep the tool cutting and shaping the bowl. A loose, flexible stance is helpful. Practice this; when it's working well, it's really fun.

Position the faceplate and screws; tap the screws in until they "bite" the wood, so they won't skip out of position.

I have removed the faceplate and will now place it on the foot. I use shorter screws here. The holes are inside what will become the shaped foot, and so will be turned away as I go. I always leave roughed-out bowls fairly thick so I will have plenty of design options when it's time to do the finish turning. Therefore I generally just eyeball the position of the faceplate on the foot. The bowl will warp in drying anyhow, so as long as it's thick enough to allow for turning into round after drying, the centering of the faceplate doesn't have to be perfect. It should be fairly close, though.

Drive the screws. Please note: you may need to drill a pilot hole to keep the base of the piece from splitting when you drive the screws in. The need for this step will vary with the type of wood, how green it is, how close the hole is to the edge of the foot, and so on. You can play it safe and pre-drill, or go for high adventure like I do.

I'm checking how far the screws protrude from the faceplate, to be certain the holes don't go too deep to be turned away when I hollow out the foot. The point of the screw looks to be at about the level of the body of the bowl, so there will be enough thickness for the screws. If the screws are too long and you don't have shorter ones, put washers on the screw between the head and the faceplate to shorten their effective length.

Mount the bowl on the lathe.

Begin by flattening the top surface, from the outside in. The tool position is now reversed; i.e., the flute is pointing to the right, and you are cutting with the long edge to the right of the tool tip.

Establish the wall thickness. As the roughed-out bowl dries, it will warp out-of-round. The degree will depend on many variables: species, drying conditions, shape and size, and so on. The bowl must be thick enough to allow for turning it back into round when you finish turn it. This bowl is about 10" in diameter; I will leave it about 1 1/4" thick. The thickness should be proportional to the overall size and diameter of the bowl. A larger bowl should be left thicker.

Begin hollowing the bowl.

A close-up of the tool as used for this cut. The flute is turned to the right, and cutting takes place along the side of the gouge to the right of the tip.

 **SAFETY TIP**

When working near the center like this, it is important to maintain control of the tool. Move steadily in toward the center, but don't push too hard. If you are leaning too hard on the tool, when it reaches the center you may inadvertently push it on into the far side of the hollow. This wall is moving upward, and will grab the tool and pull it violently upward and over, and slam it back down onto the tool rest (and perhaps your fingers).

All this happens in a fraction of the time it takes you to blink. So use caution at this point. With your left hand stationary and holding the tool firmly down against the rest, lever the tool into the center, rather than pushing it across. This levering action will allow you better control.

The hollowing cut starts at the outside circumference of the hollow...

and flows...

into the center.

SAFETY TIP

As you remove material, keep moving the tool rest closer to the work. It should be as close as possible. Always check for clearance and tighten all levers before turning on the lathe.

Again, as you approach the center, move the tool very carefully. If it slips past the center, it can be thrown violently back toward you.

The completed, roughed-out bowl. You've started with a big chunk of green wood, which would at best be difficult and very time-consuming to dry (and practically speaking, impossible); you've turned it into a bowl-shaped board of 1 1/4" or so in thickness which is easily dried.

After removing the bowl from the lathe and taking off the faceplate, I mark the bottom with the date and the type of wood.

I coat the inside end-grain as well.

Often all that's necessary at this point is to set the bowl aside for a few months to dry. However, sometimes the moisture loss is still rapid enough to cause some cracking. Many variables are involved; the type of wood and moisture content at turning, humidity and temperature in the drying location, and so forth. You may wish to seal the end grain areas of the bowl. This will slow the moisture loss from these areas, allowing the bowl to dry more evenly and preventing cracks. Here I am using Sealtite 60, diluted about 1:1 with water. If you use the full strength sealer, it will take longer to dry the piece. You want to slow the moisture loss only to the degree necessary to prevent cracking. I apply the mixture only to the vulnerable end-grain areas; coating the whole bowl would increase the drying time needlessly.

Knots and burly areas are coated with full-strength sealer, as they are very prone to cracking.

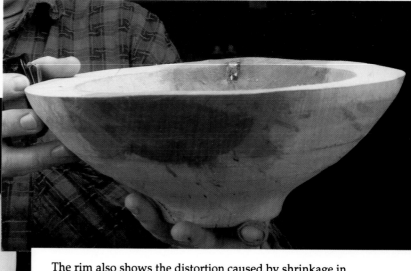

The rim also shows the distortion caused by shrinkage in drying. Now that the wood has dried and is more or less stable, you can turn the bowl to its finished diameter and thickness and it will maintain its shape. This is why you must rough-turn green wood and let it dry before finish turning if you want a round bowl when you are finished.

This Beech blank has been drying for about seven months and is ready to turn. If you look carefully, you can see how it has warped during drying. The initially round turning is now 10" in diameter across the grain

Find the center for mounting the faceplate. Sometimes, if the warpage isn't too great, you can use the same screw holes to re-mount the (same) faceplate.

and 10 1/2" in diameter with the grain.

Often, as here, the holes have moved too much, so I'll have to re-mount the faceplate with new holes. Since the wood is fairly hard, and the holes will be close to the edge, I'll pre-drill the screw holes. This will prevent splitting off part of the foot. I mark the location of the holes with the faceplate in position.

I make a quick depth-gauge by holding the drill bit next to the screw as it protrudes from the faceplate...

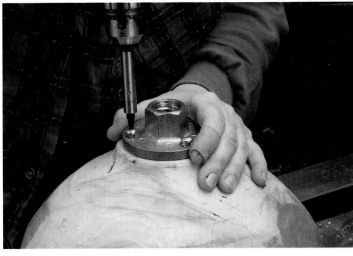

Fasten the faceplate to the bowl. Start all the screws before driving any home; this will prevent one of the screws from pulling the faceplate off-center as it is tightened.

and mark the length on the bit with a small piece of tape.

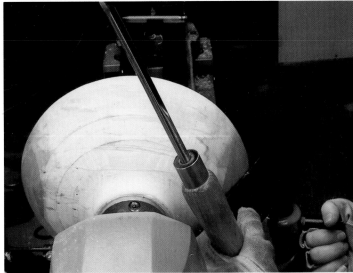

Mount the bowl on the lathe. Set the tool rest along the back side of the bowl, at or a little above the center line.

Drill the holes in the foot to the correct depth.

SAFETY TIP

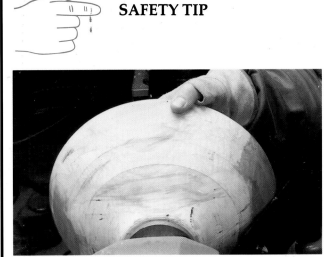

Turn the piece around and check for clearance. Be sure to turn it all the way around; remember, the bowl is wider one way than the other.

Begin by turning the bowl to round. You don't need to think about shaping or finishing cuts right now; you're just getting rid of unevenness.

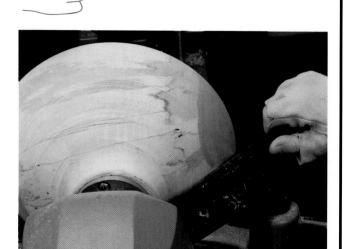

SAFETY TIP

Keep the tool rest close to the work. Remember to check for clearance. Do this even after the bowl is round. In this position, the left end of the tool rest is close to the faceplate, so you need to ensure that the screws or other parts of the faceplate and lathe will not strike the tool rest.

This is the cutting angle used to bring the bowl into round. The part of the edge doing the cutting is just to the right of the tip; the cutting edge forms an angle of roughly 45 degrees to the wood approaching the tool. (Don't go get your protractors! That's just an approximation! It means, "Somewhere in between parallel and perpendicular, not too close to either extreme." Hey, if you're into absolutes, cut some dovetails...). This cut removes a fair amount of wood and leaves a reasonably clean surface.

For finer shaping and a more finished surface, I move the tool to this position. The long edge on the right side of the gouge (here hidden behind the left edge; the flute is pointed toward the right) is doing the cutting. The cutting edge is nearly parallel with the rotation of the wood. This slices off a very fine shaving and leaves a very clean surface.

Start at the bottom of the foot, and move upward toward the body of the bowl.

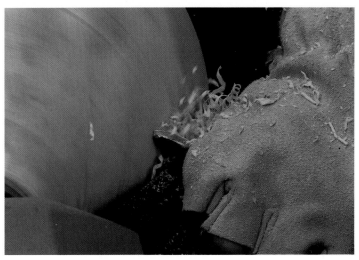

To control the shape, twist the handle of the gouge as you move it across the surface. Note the long, fine, clean shavings. When you see shavings like these, you know you are getting a nice, smooth cut on the bowl.

Work your way up the side of the bowl. It may feel "backward" to cut in this direction, but cutting "uphill" (that is, from smaller to larger diameter) on the outside of the bowl will result in a much cleaner surface than cutting "downhill". Turning from smaller to larger diameter means there is always wood just ahead of the wood being cut. Thus the fibers are supported from behind, and the tool can slice through them cleanly. Cutting "downhill" allows the wood fibers to be pushed out into the empty space ahead of the cut, resulting in tearing and pulling of the fibers, and a rougher surface.

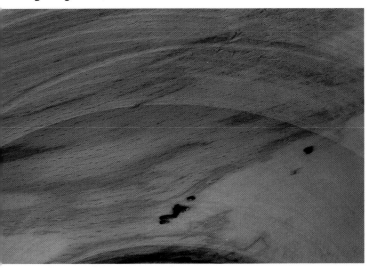

Notice the clean surface obtained on the foot of the bowl with the finishing cut. Compare to the body of the bowl as the roughing cut has left it.

This surface still needs to be refined, as there is considerable tear-out from the roughing cuts. It is nearly impossible to sand through this kind of tearing--it is far better to learn to use the cutting tools properly and leave a good surface.

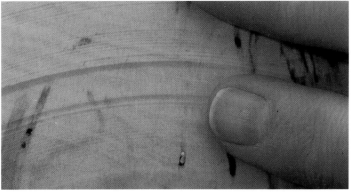

Begin to smooth and shape the body of the bowl. With the lathe stopped, I have turned the bowl by hand with the tool held in position to show you what the cut looks like. The handle of the tool is held very low, and the tool is almost straight up and down. This brings the long side edge nearly parallel with the rotating wood. In this position, the edge slices cleanly through the wood and leaves a very satisfactory surface which will not require a lot of sanding.

I will try to eliminate these ridges, too. But they are much less of a problem than the tearing, because they are easily sanded off. Compare the quality of this surface to the one in the previous photo. In spite of the ridges, the surface is basically clean.

29

Continue refining the surface, working from foot to rim. (Just look at those cute little shavings!)

Another useful technique for finishing the outside of the bowl uses a scraper to make what is generally called a shear-scraping cut. The actual cutting is done by a wire edge, or burr, which is raised on the top of the tool. (See sharpening section, pages 11-13.)

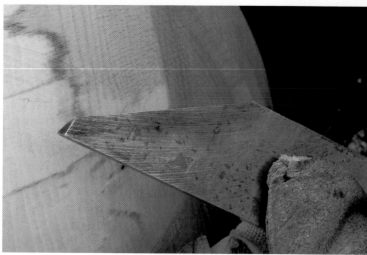

You will most likely find it necessary to change the position of the toolrest to keep it close to the work.

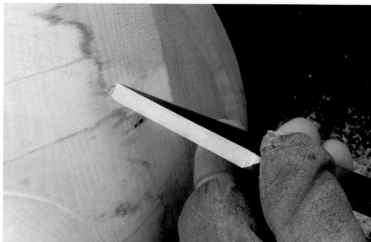

The bevel of the tool.

   **SAFETY TIP**

Do this with the lathe turned off, and double check for clearance and that the levers are all tight before turning the machine back on.

You may also need to change the placement of your hands and the tool. Remember, you are after getting the edge into the right position to make a clean cut. Reason backward (or outward) from there and hold the tool handle as necessary to accomplish this.

The angle of the tool is critical in this cut. Perpendicular to the direction of rotation, as shown in this photo, would give a very aggressive (hence not very clean) cut.

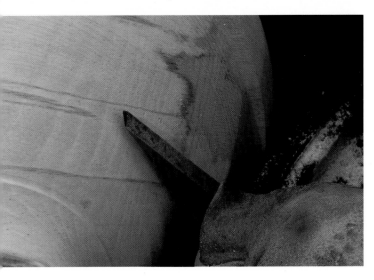

Directly in line with the rotation it will not cut at all.

but will have a strong tendency to kick back.

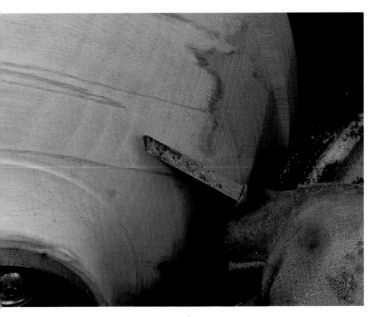

The cut is made between these extremes.

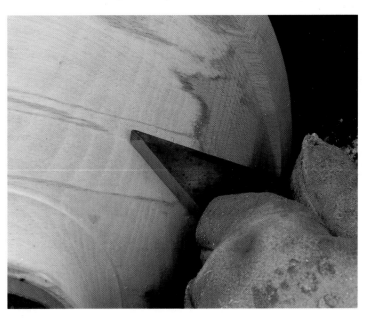

This angle (again, exaggerated for clarity), while much safer, will not cut very well. So again, the cut is made...

The other operative angle is the angle between the flat of the tool and the surface of the bowl. This angle (exaggerated for clarity) with a lot of distance between the tool surface and the wood, will cut very aggressively...

with the tool held somewhere in between these extremes. Remember to work in an uphill direction. This cut is very delicate; it's more like stroking the bowl than cutting it. You are cutting with that tiny burr which you can't even see. If you are too forceful or aggressive you'll just ruin the tool edge and tear the wood. This cut is for final finishing and very subtle shape refinement. If you need to remove a lot of material, go back to the gouge.

SAFETY TIP

Be sure you keep the tip of the tool high enough off the work to prevent it catching and digging into the rotating wood.

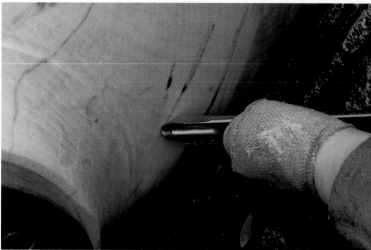

Slowly bring the edge toward the wood by swinging the tool handle around...

Used properly, this cut will result in very fine shavings, not dust.

until the edge engages the wood. Then gently bring the tool forward, taking a very light cut...

As I've said, it's best to go uphill on the outside of the bowl. This cuts more cleanly through the fibers. Occasionally it's not possible to do this. To clean up the area just beside the foot as shown here, there is not enough room to get the tool in and cut uphill. Over small distances like this you can sometimes get away with cutting downhill. Use the small, pointed spindle gouge for this. Take a very light cut with a very sharp tool. Move slowly and carefully. You also need to blend the cut into the surface of the bowl. To do this, and to avoid cutting too aggressively initially, begin by holding the bevel of the gouge against the work, with the edge completely off the wood. (The lathe is stopped in the photo for clarity).

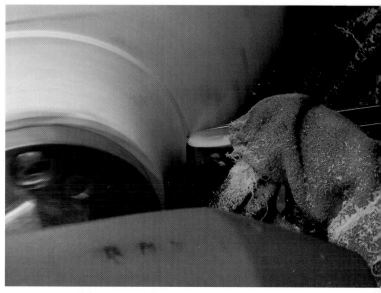

back to the fillet on the foot.

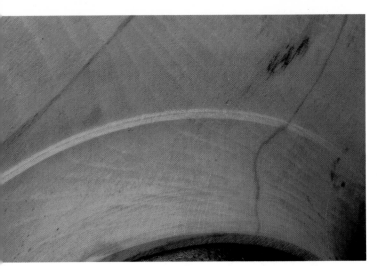

This fillet separates and defines the segments. With the surface next to it cleanly cut, it'll be easier to sand. Heavy sanding would round over the fillet and spoil the nice, crisp detail.

I can't get all the way up under the rim with the shear-scraping cut, so I use the small spindle gouge again. This is the same cut just used next to the foot, only the direction is reversed. This time I'll be cutting uphill, so a clean cut will be easy.

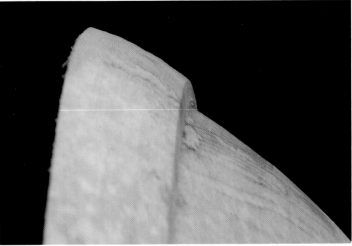

I make a final cut on the fillet to clean it up.

Note the little bump or ridge left on the curve of the bowl where I began the finish cut under the rim. This often happens when switching in mid-curve from one tool or type of cut to another. The break in the curve is displeasing to the eye and hand even if the mind doesn't specifically register it. Fixing these little problems makes the difference between a mediocre and a really fine bowl.

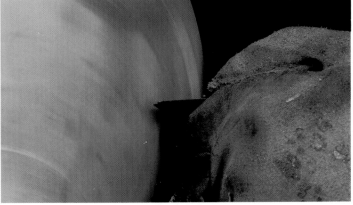

Using the scraper for a shear-scraping cut, blend the area you just cut into the body of the bowl.

I go back to the scraper, again using the shear-scraping cut, to blend in the area.

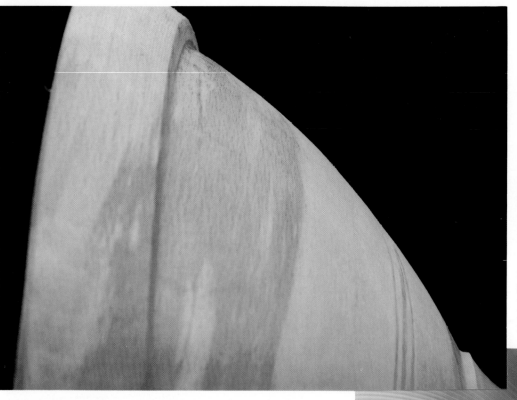

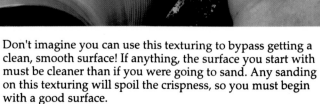

Start at the foot, and work up to the rim. You have to concentrate to get the cuts even. If some are much heavier or further apart than others, it won't look right.

Now the curve flows smoothly from the foot to the rim.

I often texture part of the bowl. This provides a pleasing contrast. Here I will use the small spindle gouge for maneuverability.

Don't imagine you can use this texturing to bypass getting a clean, smooth surface! If anything, the surface you start with must be cleaner than if you were going to sand. Any sanding on this texturing will spoil the crispness, so you must begin with a good surface.

The texture is made by cutting a series of concentric grooves all along the side of the bowl. Notice the angle of the tool. It is cutting just to the right of the tip.

Bring the toolrest in closer as you move up the side of the bowl. Continue cutting up to the rim.

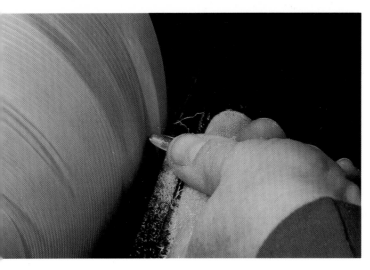

Smooth the underside of the fillet at the rim with a slow, delicate finish cut.

Move the tool rest close to the rim and begin shaping it.

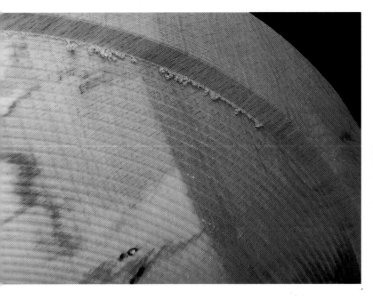

This has left a few wood fibers standing.

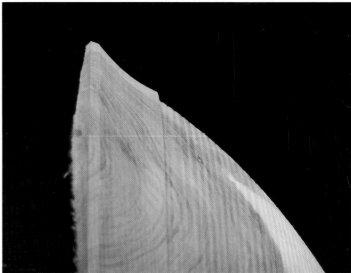

I've made the outside of the rim concave to pick up on the shape of the foot.

Come back up the body of the bowl to slice these off. Use the very tip of the tool, and be sure not to cut into the already finished surface of the bowl body.

This scraper is designed for working on a concave surface.

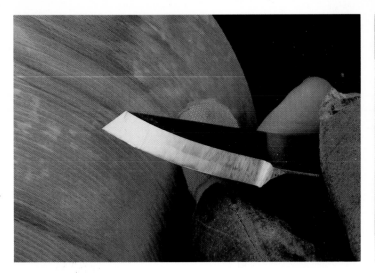

The bevel of the tool. I'll use this to make the delicate shear-scraping cut on the rim.

Taking a very light cut, work from bottom to top.

Move the tool rest around to the top of the bowl. Using the small bowl gouge, and cutting from the outside edge in, begin by facing off the still-uneven rim.

Cut back toward the rim on the inside of the bowl to bring it into round. Take light cuts, as the uneven surface makes the tool tend to grab. Keep the flute of the gouge pointed toward the left, not up. The cut is less "grabby" this way.

After you have worked the rim into round, begin shaping it. I like a wide rim; with food in the bowl it's like a frame on a picture. Also it shows off the wood to good effect, and is a pleasing contrast to the thinner wall of the bowl.

I left a small lip on the inside of the rim.

There is some tearing on the lip...

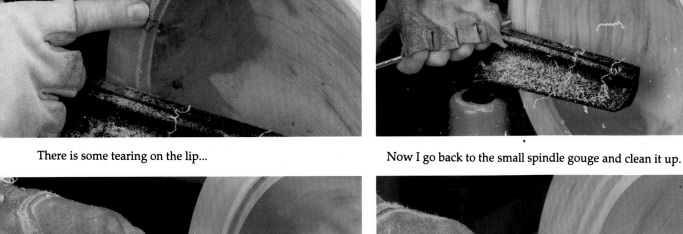

Now I go back to the small spindle gouge and clean it up.

so I'll re-cut it.

To smoothly cut the beaded lip, start at the top of the bead...

and cut down one side.

The roughed-out rim. Note that although this is just the initial shaping, you should be aiming for fairly clean cuts. You don't want to have tearing too deep for the finish cuts to remove easily. Also the lip and edge are vulnerable to breakage if you cut too forcefully when shaping.

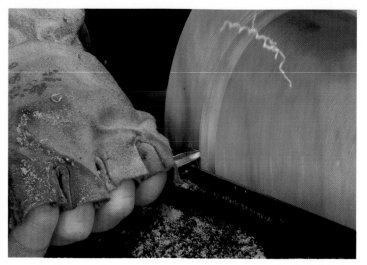

Return to the top...

and blend it in to the curved sides already established.

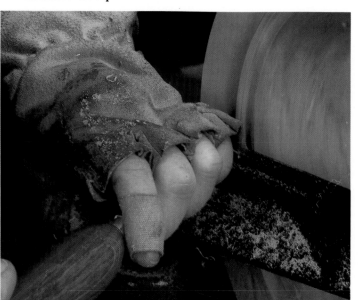

and cut down the other side.

Move the tool rest close to the interior of the bowl. Using the small bowl gouge, I'll work the top of the bowl to finished thickness before working on down deeper in the bowl; this leaves as much mass as possible in the bowl to support the piece while cutting. I'll go only about to here in the first stage.

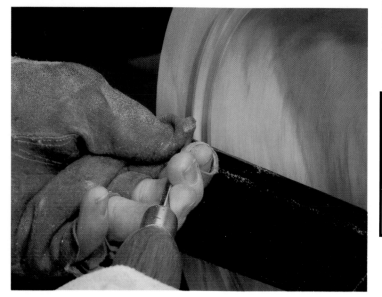

It's easy to let the bead get too pointed on top, and indeed I have done, so I'll flatten the top a bit...

 **SAFETY TIP**

Remember to check for clearance——the inside of the bowl is not yet round.

PLACE
STAMP
HERE

SCHIFFER PUBLISHING LTD
77 LOWER VALLEY RD
ATGLEN PA 19310-9717

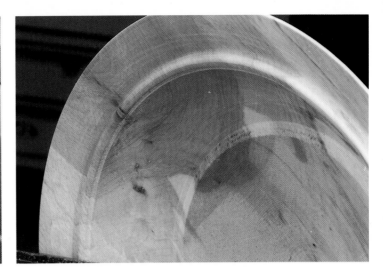

Here, I am close to the finished thickness. The inside surface of the bowl will begin just at the beaded lip. Notice on the wide part of the rim there is a bit of chattering. This was caused by vibration of the relatively thin rim of the bowl and of the gouge during final cutting. It's not a major problem because it's relatively easy to fix—as long as it's clean (no tearing of the wood fibers) and doesn't go too close in to the bead (where it would be difficult to sand without ruining the bead).

Start the final, finishing cut with a sharp tool and with the tool rest as close in as possible. Begin at the lip...

Work your way down the side, adjusting the angle of the tool as necessary to keep the bevel rubbing and to follow the curve. The tool rest should be at or just a bit below center.

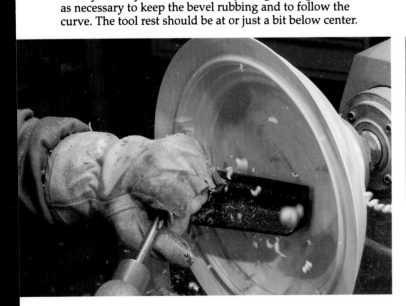

Take fairly light cuts as you approach the final thickness. Tear-out on the interior is most difficult to eliminate.

and cut down into the bowl, stopping just a little before you reach the still-irregular part of the wall. This will allow you to work gradually back to this finished surface as you work the next section, making it easier to blend the curves.

Notice my left hand behind the piece, giving some support to the bowl. This helps dampen the vibration that develops as the wall gets thinner. It only takes a very light pressure to do this; hold on too tightly and your hand will get burned!

The upper part of the interior being finished, begin working down the side into the bottom. It's not a finish cut at this stage, but...

This double-ended caliper can also be used to check wall thickness, and will reach farther than your fingers. Note that I have taped a little foam to the tip that will pass over the finished outside surface of the bowl.

it's not a deep roughing-out cut either. Remember that tear-out on the inside of the bowl is nearly impossible to fix. Take light, clean cuts as you work toward the final surface.

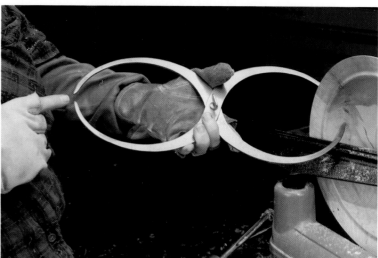

Use the tool like this. The gap at the outside end shows the thickness being measured at the bowl.

You can check for thickness and evenness of the curve with your fingers, as far down the side as you can reach.

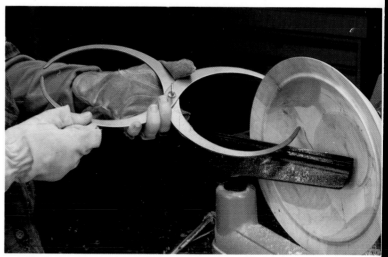

Slide the caliper gently on down the side of the bowl. You're aiming for a consistent thickness from the bottom of the rim area all the way down to the foot.

WE HOPE THAT YOU ENJOY THIS BOOK . . . and that it will occupy a proud place in your library. We would like to keep you informed about other publications from Schiffer

Go back over the inside, bringing down the thicker areas.

It thickens just about here, so I know where to begin blending when I go in to make the next series of cuts.

The finishing cut should be as clean as possible, and should blend the surface into one smooth continuous curve.

The long overhang of the tool from the rest to the bottom of the bowl begins to be a problem. There is too much vibration to cut well. One way to solve this is to switch to a bigger tool with more mass to dampen vibration. It's that supporting mass that warrants the use of this larger tool here--you're still making small, clean cuts with it.

Keep checking the wall thickness.

The side is finished to about this point, having even thickness, a smooth curve, and a clean surface.

I begin working in toward the center, still using the larger tool for support.

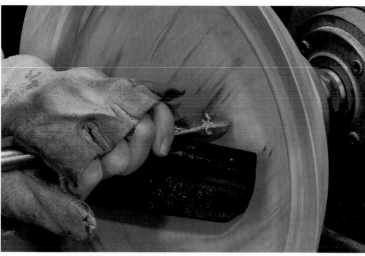

The final passes should be very fine cuts.

As you approach the center, working the surface down, there will be a nub left in the middle.

Check the thickness again.

Remove this in stages, with light cuts. If you try to cut off the entire thickness at once, the whole nub may just break off and pull out fibers from below the finished surface, leaving a mess that's difficult or impossible to fix.

For the final blending, I start out here where I will not actually be removing any wood. This will help make the curve nice and smooth. Riding back on the bevel of the tool, I establish the arc of motion...

and move in toward the center...

In this position, if the tool catches in the wood...

until the edge of the gouge engages the wood. The smooth curve created will not disappoint eye or hand.

it will be thrown away from the wood. If the rest were below center, the tool would be pulled into the wood, causing damage to the bowl definitely, and to you possibly.

A large heavy scraper is sometimes useful to further refine the inside surface. Position the rest above center.

In using this tool, remember to maintain fine control and cut very lightly. You are cutting with that microscopic burr edge you have so carefully established (pages 11-13). All the rest of that steel is there just to provide a steady support for that tiny wire edge, which will clean up small defects in the surface by taking off very fine shavings.

Hold the blade between thumb and fingers, and down against the tool rest. Your index finger rests against the back of the tool rest. Thus you can move the tool in and out with great control. Your right hand, out on the handle, controls the angle of the tool.

Again, proper use of this tool results in very fine shavings, not dust.

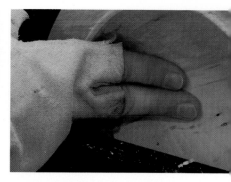

Use your finger (with the lathe stopped) to check the final surface. You can feel bumps and irregularities that you can't see. Especially if your eyes are as, shall we say, well-used, as are mine...

This bowl is ready for sanding!

Sanding the Bowl

I make my own sanding discs, but they can be bought ready-made. The back is a (worn out) quick release sanding disc, to which I have glued a circle of 1/4" thick foam rubber.

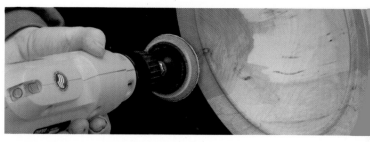

For sanding I usually slow the lathe a little from its turning speed. The drill should be high speed, around 2500 rpm, and must be reversible. This method of power sanding a turned piece is much easier and faster than simply hand sanding by holding sandpaper against the spinning work. It doesn't totally replace hand sanding, and there will be cases where that is still useful.

On top of the foam a leather disc is glued. The sandpaper circles are glued to the leather with rubber cement, and will peel off readily when worn out. I make up several at a time in each grit so I don't have to stop in the middle of sanding to replace paper. I also keep discs in a variety of sizes and made to have different degrees of aggressiveness in sanding. This way I can match the disc to the situation.

I'll start at the rim, and begin with an 80 grit disc to eliminate the chatter left from the turning. Where the sanding disc is touching the wood, it should be going in the opposite direction from the surface. In this case, that means the drill is in reverse. Start with the edge of the disc in the crease next to the lip...

move out over the slightly convex rim...

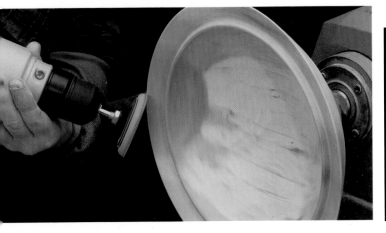

and gently round over the edge.

On the inside of the bowl the opposite side of the disc is in contact, so I reverse the direction of the drill. I also switch to a 120-grit disc, as the 80 grit isn't needed here. Work from the center...

out toward the rim. Don't stay in one place or you'll create a dip.

If there is a high spot you need to reduce, work around and into it to avoid creating a dip.

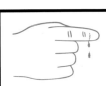

SAFETY TIP

Work in the lower left quadrant of the bowl. This way, if the spinning bowl "grabs" the disc, it will be thrown away from the wood. If this happens with the disc on the right side, it will pull the disc up into the bowl and it will kick back at you.

There is a bit of a dip right in the center. I turn the lathe off and blend it in by working all around it with the disc. With the bowl stationary, it is even more important to keep the disc moving to avoid gouging into the bowl, especially when using the more aggressive coarser grits.

With the lathe off, I've switched to a larger disc to level the bottom. The larger disc will bridge the dip and make the blending easier. The small disc tends to just follow the defect.

The bottom fixed, I work my way out to the rim, removing tool marks as I go.

Use fingers as well as eyes to check for smoothness.

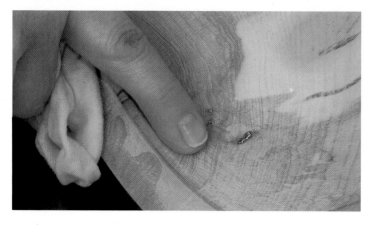

A common problem in end-grain areas is this kind of "blush." The surface feels smooth, but you can see bruising of the fibers.

Sometimes moistening the area with a little water will help. The moisture swells the wood fibers, raising the grain. After it dries...

sand again, working in both directions to slice off fibers.

When the surface is smooth and level, switch to the next finer grit and sand again. One of the keys to good sanding is not to move on to the next finer grit until you have improved the surface as much as possible with each grit. This includes not moving on until you have eliminated all sanding marks from the previous grit.

I find a good sequence of grits is 80 (when necessary for really rough areas) 120, 220, 280, 320. I turn most of my salad bowls and plates from domestic hard woods, and find 320 is fine enough for these, but you may wish to go to 400 or even higher on very dense exotics.

Sometimes you'll need to go over the end grain areas with the lathe off to get them really clean. Use a 120 or finer grit disc; the 80 grit is too aggressive to use with the lathe off. Remember, with the lathe off, it is even more crucial to keep the disc moving, or you'll create dents you can't get rid of.

Move on to 180 grit and sand again.

Until now I haven't touched the bead on the rim. The coarser grits are too aggressive and are likely to slip and mar another part of the work, or the bead itself. With the 180 I can smooth it safely.

If you have trouble getting rid of all the radial scratches from the power sanding, it can be helpful to sand with a hand held sheet. It may be necessary to go back to the previous grit, and you should slow the lathe a bit for hand sanding.

Move on through the grits. The final sanding is done with the 320 grit disc.

I usually do a final sanding with a 320 grit sheet...

followed with a micro-fine Bear-Tex™ finishing pad to polish the surface. These pads are a good substitute for steel wool-- they last longer, will not leave particles in the wood as steel wool can, and can be cut as needed with a pair of scissors.

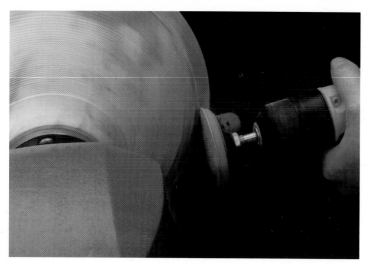

On the back of the bowl, I sand the rim...

and the foot, with the discs, starting at 120 grit. I don't use the power sanding on the textured body of the bowl; it would round over the crisp detail and spoil the effect.

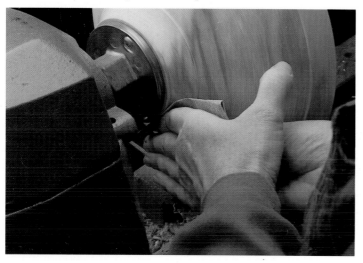

For the finer grits I'm switching to hand-held sheet paper on the foot because it's difficult to get into this spot with the disc. The important thing is to get the surface good and clean.

There is a crack on the foot of the bowl.

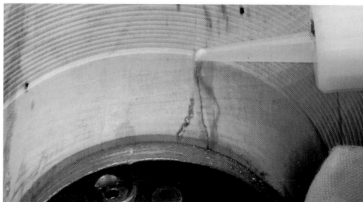

To fix it, I use cyanoacrylate glue. This comes in three thicknesses. First run a bead of the thin glue along the crack.

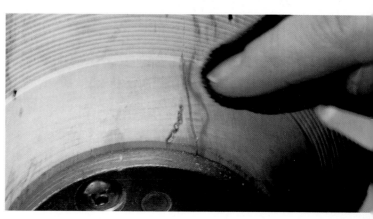

Immediately wipe away the excess.

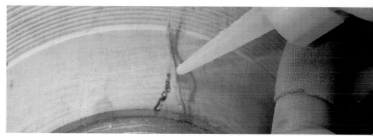

Follow this with a line of medium thickness, or "gap-filling" glue. The previous application of thin glue, which easily soaks into the crack, will help pull the thicker glue into the crack. At this point I often take a pinch of fine shavings off the lathe bed (or wherever) and rub them into the crack.

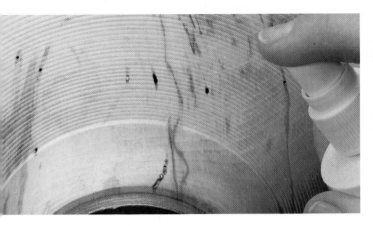

Wait a minute or so, then spray the repair with accelerator; this sets the glue very rapidly.

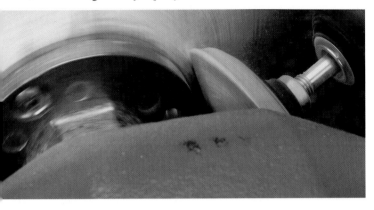

As soon as the glue is completely dry, start the lathe and sand with the disc.

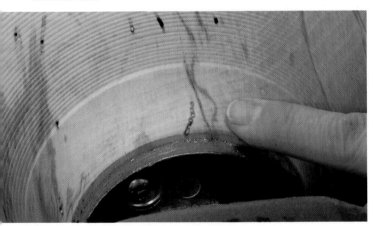

While still noticeable, the repaired crack blends with the other markings on the wood. It is definitely more sound.

After completing the sanding of the foot and rim, go over the whole surface with the Bear-Tex™ pad.

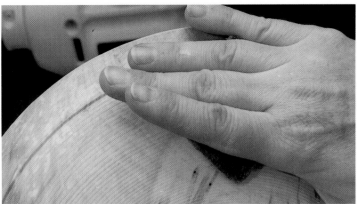

If your lathe reverses, go over the whole bowl with the Bear-Tex™ pad while the lathe spins in reverse. If it doesn't, stop the lathe and rub by hand with the pad in the direction opposite rotation. This will take off the microscopic fibers left lying in the direction of rotation, and give a surface smooth to the fingers as well as the eye.

Judy's Low-Tech, Fun-N-Easy-to-Make, So-Nontoxic-You-Could-Eat-It-in-a-Famine Plate, Platter and Salad Bowl Finish.

On functional bowls, platters, and plates--any piece which will be used to contain food--I use a mixture of beeswax and walnut oil which I make myself. I like this mixture for several reasons. It is easy to apply, and is totally non-toxic (unless you happen to be allergic to beeswax or walnuts) at all stages. It is also easy to repair, and it leaves the bowl with a nice smooth feel.

This recipe uses a proportion of one part wax to 8 parts oil, by weight. You may wish to play around with the amounts: more wax = harder mixture; more oil = softer.

To make the mixture, melt 5 oz. of beeswax in the top of a double boiler. Pour 40 oz. of walnut oil, a little at a time, into the melted wax. Stir gently after each addition until the wax (which has hardened somewhat on contact with the cool oil) is melted again. This part is pretty fun--with the addition of the cooler oil to the melted wax, some of the wax congeals into amazing forms. It's really cool; if you have kids or grandkids in the house, they will definitely want to see this! Continue until all the oil is added.

You can easily check the final consistency of your mixture. Just pour a spoonful into a small cup. It will quickly cool and you can decide whether you like the consistency. If it's too soft, add a little wax; too hard, more oil.

Don't overheat the mixture. You don't want to cook it, just to mix the two ingredients thoroughly. As soon as all the oil is added and the wax melted back in, remove from heat and pour into small containers--old cottage cheese or tofu tubs work well. Store containers not in use in the refrigerator or freezer. They'll keep indefinitely.

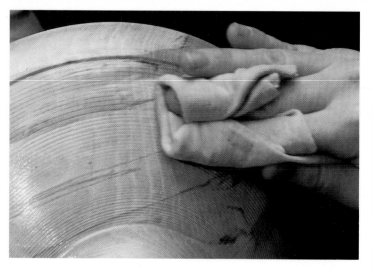

With the lathe stopped, use a clean rag to apply a thick coat of finish to the bowl. Cover the entire surface as quickly as possible; some woods will show streaking if the initial coat doesn't go on virtually all at once.

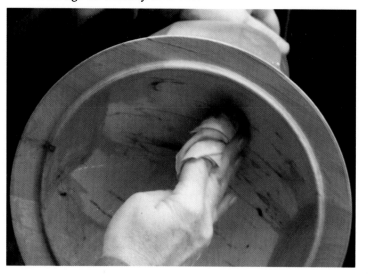

Do the same on the inside....

and the rim.

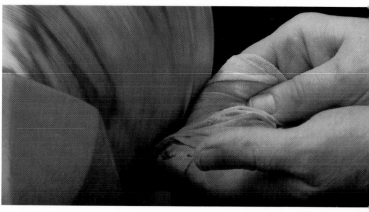

Turn the lathe on and work the finish into the surface.

Let it rest for a few minutes so the wood will soak up more of the finish. Then turn the lathe back on and go over the entire bowl with a dry, clean cloth.

This removes any excess and polishes the bowl.

Remove from the lathe, and take off the faceplate.

Almost finished!

Mount the faceplate on the center of one of the discs.

⟨BUILDING A JIG FOR TURNING THE FOOT⟩

Draw a circle, of the largest diameter that will clear the bed of your lathe, on each of two pieces of 3/4" plywood.

Place the assembly on the lathe.

Cut them out.

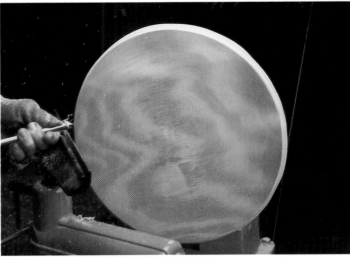

Round over the edges, so you won't chew up your arm or hand if you brush up against it while it's spinning.

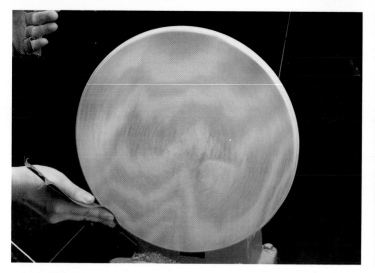

Sand with coarse sand paper.

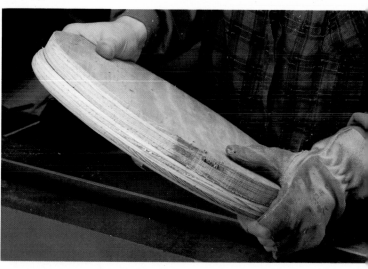

and press the two circles together.

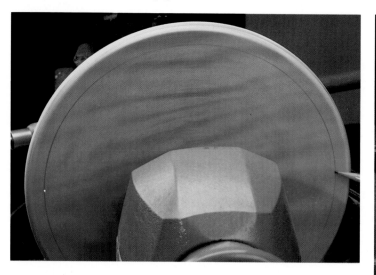

On the back, with the lathe running, draw a line near the edge for the holes to be drilled. The line should be far enough in from the edge that the bolts can't break through the edge, but the circle must be larger than the bowl you will be holding in the jig.

Make four marks equidistant on the circle.

I'll drill both discs at the same time and I want the holes to line up. So to hold the discs together, I apply double faced carpet tape to one surface,

At each point marked, drill holes large enough for a 3/8" bolt (I use a drill bit 1/32" over size, to prevent binding of the bolts when loading the jig).

We need a large hole in the center of the second disc. An easy way to create this is on the lathe. Bolt the discs together, using 3/8" carriage screws and wing nuts. Crank the wing nuts nice and tight to seat the square neck of the bolt in the wood. It's easier to do this now than with a bowl in the jig.

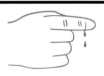
SAFETY TIP

Always have the bolts protrude on the back, or faceplate side, of the jig so they will be toward the machine and away from tender knuckles.

Mount the assembly on the lathe.

SAFETY TIP

Check for clearance of the bolts with the machine in back and with the tool rest in front.

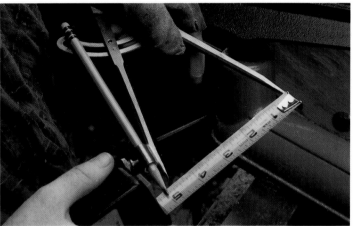

Set a compass or caliper to approximately 5", or a little larger than the diameter of the foot on your bowl.

Use the compass to transfer this measurement to the spinning disc.

SAFETY TIP

ONLY the pencil should actually touch the wood. The pointed end on the right is for sighting only. If it touches the wood it will be flung up and over and can cause injury.

Turn the hole, beginning at the circumference. I use the small bowl gouge for this.

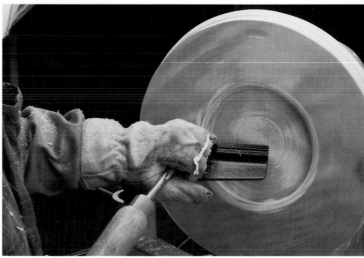

Take the bolts out, turn the donut circle over, re-mount, and turn off the sharp edge of the hole. Taper it gently like the other side, and sand smooth. The jig is finished!

When you've cut all the way through, the center will pop out.

To load the jig, begin by laying a circle of soft foam rubber (a scrap of carpet foam works fine) on the solid disc. The bowl goes on top of this, rim down.

Clean up the hole. The edge should taper from the surface of the disk into the center of the wood. Sand it smooth.

A ring of foam protects the bowl.

The donut circle goes on top.

With the assembly mounted on the lathe, rotate the piece by hand and note how far it is off-center. I use my thumb held down on the tool rest for a reference point.

Choose bolts long enough to join the jig, but not so long as to protrude too far from the back of the jig. Turn the wing nuts down lightly. You need to leave it loose enough to center the bowl before turning.

As you turn the assembly, the gap will widen or narrow.

Ready to mount on the lathe and center.

Gently push or tap the bowl until you have it perfectly centered. Then tighten all the wing nuts firmly down. Set the tool rest, and spin by hand again to check for clearance. I use the small bowl gouge to rough out the foot.

To begin, I'll turn enough to get rid of the screw holes; that's a technical consideration. Aesthetically, I envision the center of the foot to be a continuation of the wall of the bowl. It should look and feel as though the foot ring was applied to a smooth, continuously curved surface.

Switch to a spindle gouge for the finishing cuts. Make a fine finishing cut across the outside edge of the foot ring. Cut from the outside in; this way any minor tear-out at the edge will be eliminated as you cut the inside wall.

Stop the lathe and check occasionally for depth.

You may need to gently round over the outside edge if the bottom cut has left it sharp.

The foot ring is roughed out. Keep the tool rest close in, always double checking that it's tight before starting the lathe again.

Using a light finishing cut, clean up the inside wall of the foot ring.

Work toward the finished surface in the bottom of the foot. Remember, you want the curve to match the line of the wall of the bowl.

Again, I work from the center outward. The flute of the gouge is pointing to the left.

For the final finishing cut, work from the center out to the edge. This keeps you cutting in the right direction to slice the fibers cleanly.

When the texturing is complete, sand the foot. I usually do this only with hand sanding. The discs are aggressive and hard to control in the confined spaces of the foot.

Having established the shape and a clean surface, switch to the small spindle gouge to create the textured cut as on the side of the bowl.

Start with 80 or 120 grit as needed, but don't touch the ridges until you're using 220 or 280 grit, or you'll spoil the crisp texture.

When sanding is complete, polish with the Bear-Tex™ pad.

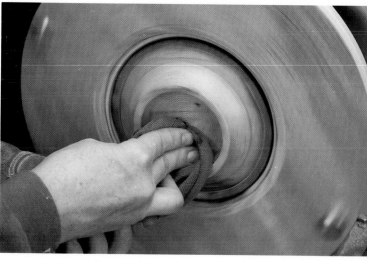

Let it rest for a few minutes, then buff with a clean dry cloth.

Apply the finish with a cloth....

A nicely finished foot. A bowl has a "bottom" only because it is three-dimensional and therefore must sit somewhere. Being three-dimensional, it doesn't have a "back" - a place that doesn't matter. A poorly made foot is a disappointment to the eye and hand of the person who troubles to pick a piece up and look at it. The foot should receive the same careful attention to design and finishing that you have lavished upon the rest of the piece.

and work it into the surface with the bowl spinning.

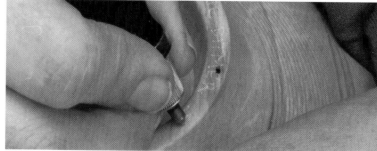

All that's left is to sign the piece. I do this with an electric engraver. It makes a legible, permanent line that is not too obtrusive.

I like to mark the work with my name, the wood and the date.

No doubt some of you will notice this is beech, not sycamore. I don't know why I wrote sycamore on there, but I like to imagine it makes the piece more valuable - like a mis-struck coin...

The completed bowl.

Detail of the foot. (And if you missed it in the text--yep, I know it's not sycamore, it's beech!)

 CONCLUSION

Now go forth and make a hundred more of them.

Detail of the rim.

Bowl, Figured Maple. 6" height x 9" diameter.

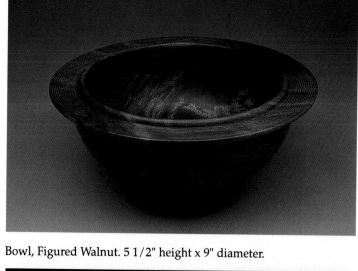

Bowl, Figured Walnut. 5 1/2" height x 9" diameter.

Bowl, Sycamore. 5" height x 13" diameter.

Bowl, Cherry. 3" height x 13 1/2" diameter.

Bowl, cherry. 6 1/2" height x 9" diameter.

Clockwise from top right:
Bowl, Cherry. 7" height x 9 1/2" diameter.
Bowl, Maple. 4 1/2" height x 14" diameter.
Plate, Mayan Bloodwood. 9 1/2" diameter.
Platter, Ash. 16" diameter.

Plates. Clockwise from top left, ending in center:
    Maple, 10 1/2" diameter.
    Goncalo Alves, 7" diameter.
    Oak, 7" diameter.
    Goncalo Alves, 7 1/2" diameter.
    Oak, 6" diameter.

Plates; Cherry, Maple. 6-8" diameter.

Plates. Clockwise from top:
    Goncalo Alves, 7" diameter.
    Goncalo Alves, 7 1/2" diameter.
    Oak, 7" diameter.

The pieces in this section have arisen out of a continuing exploration of bowl-turning. I hope seeing them will encourage your own investigation.

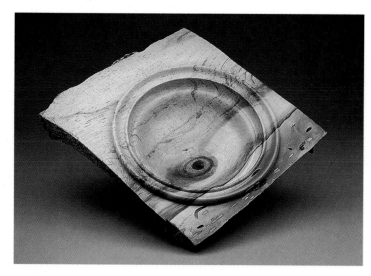

Sculptural Bowl, Persimmon. 3" height x 13" width x 15" depth.

Sculptural Bowl, Jarrah Burl. 6 1/4" height x 9" width x 9 1/2" depth.

Sculptural Bowl, Jarrah. 5 1/4" height x 15" width X 12 3/4" depth.

Platter, Walnut. 2" height x 11 1/2" width x 14 1/2" depth.

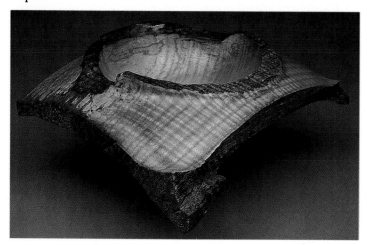

Sculptural Bowl, Figured Ash. 4 1/2" height x 9 1/2" width x 8" depth.

Sculptural Bowl, Australian (?). 3 1/8" height x 6 5/8" width x 6 3/8" depth.

Detail

Sculptural Bowl, Figured Ash. 3 3/4" height x 9 1/2" width x 8" depth.

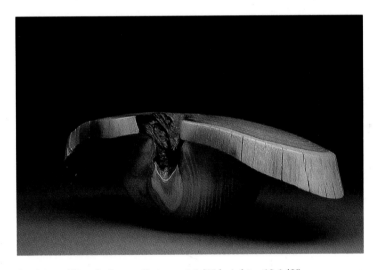

Sculptural Bowl, Osage Orange. 4 1/2" height x 13 1/2" width x 8 1/2" depth.

Sculptural Bowl, Cherry. 3 1/2" height x 12" width x 11 1/2" depth.

Sculptural Bowl, Cedar. 3 1/4" height x 7 1/4" width x 6" depth.

Sculptural Bowl, Persimmon. 3" height x 11" width x 10" depth.

Sculptural Bowl, Spalted Beech. 5 1/2" height x 7" diameter.

Sculptural Bowl, Mulberry. 4" height x 5" diameter.

Be prepared...
To learn...
To succeed...

Get **REA**dy. It all starts here.
REA's preparation for the HSPA Mathematics
is **fully aligned** with the Core Curriculum
Content Standards adopted by the New Jersey
Department of Education.

Free!
2 Practice Tests Online
www.rea.com/HSPA

*Visit us online at **www.rea.com***